A SHAMBHALA THRESHOLD BOOK

10.95

OPEN SECRET
Versions of Rumi

Translated by John Moyne and Coleman Barks

SHAMBHALA
Boston & London
1999

SHAMBHALA PUBLICATIONS, INC.
Horticultural Hall
300 Massachusetts Avenue
Boston, Massachusetts 02115
www.shambhala.com

9 8 7 6 5 4 3 2
Printed in the United States of America
⊚ This edition is printed on acid-free paper
that meets the American National Standards Institute Z39.48 Standard.
Distributed in the United States by Random House, Inc.,
and in Canada by Random House of Canada Ltd

Some of these versions have appeared in the Yellow Moon Press publication
Night and Sleep, and in *Plainsong* and *Epos* magazines.

Library of Congress Cataloging-in-Publications Data

Jalāl al-Dīn Rūmī, Maulana, 1207–1273

       [Selections. English. 1999]
       Open secret: versions of Rumi/translated by John Moyne and
Coleman Barks.
             p.   cm.
       Includes bibliographical references (p. ix.).
       ISBN 1–57062–529–8 (pbk.)
        1. Jalāl al-Dīn Rūmī, Maulana, 1207–1273 Translations into
English. I. Moyne, John. II. Barks, Coleman. III. Title.
PK6480.E5M6   1999   CIP
891'.5511—dc21   99–31399

This book is dedicated to everyone
who opens it.

"In these pages many mysteries are hinted at.
 What if you come to understand one of them?"

"Words let water from an unseen, infinite ocean
 Come into this place as energy for the dying and even the dead."

"Bored onlookers, but with such Light in our eyes!
 As we read this book, the jewel-lights intensify."

—Rumi

CONTENTS

A Note on the Translations

These are collaborative translations. John Moyne translates from the Persian of Rumi, and Coleman Barks works with the literal translations, trying to be faithful to the tone, as he hears it, and the images. Some of these are reworkings of translations done much earlier by Arberry and Nicholson.

The short poems (Quatrains) are all John Moyne–Coleman Barks translations. Among the Odes the following are Moyne–Barks collaborations: #425, #617, #805, #810, #950, #959, #1051, #1101, #1370, and "Who Says Words with My Mouth."

Arberry–Barks versions: #1692, #1739, #1754, #1850, #1861, #1937, #2015, #2110, #2157, #2172, #2180, #2195, #2232, #2253, #2345, #2389, #2412, #2422, #2465, #2498, #2522, #2537, #2558, #2674, #2693, #2776, #2788, #2873, #2933, #3019, #3061, #3071.

Nicholson–Barks versions: "The Music," "Display," "The Question," "The Variety of Intelligence in Human Beings," "Why Organize a Universe This Way?" "Learning the Signs of the Zodiac," "Those You Are With," and "The Name."

References:

Furuzanfar, Badi-uz-Zaman. *Kulliyat-e Shams,* 8 vols., Tehran: Amir Kabir Press, 1957–66. Critical edition of the collected odes, quatrains, and other poems of Rumi with glossary and notes.

Arberry, A. J. *Mystical Poems of Rumi.* Persian Heritage Series No. 3. Chicago: The University of Chicago Press, 1968. Translation of 200 odes taken from the Furuzanfar edition, with notes.

Arberry, A. J. *Mystical Poems of Rumi.* Persian Heritage Series No. 23. Boulder, Colorado: Westview Press, 1979. Translation of a further 200 odes taken from the Furuzanfar edition.

Nicholson, R. A. *The Mathnawi of Jalaluddin Rumi.* 8 vols. London: Luzac & Co., 1925–40. Critical edition, translation, and commentary.

Introduction

Rumi's Life (1207-1273)

Jelaluddin Rumi was born in Balkh, in what is now Afghanistan, on September 30, 1207. When he was still a young man, though, his family fled under the threat of a Mongol invasion, and after much traveling, finally settled in Konya, Turkey. *Rumi* means "the Roman," that is, "from Roman Anatolia."

Rumi followed in the line of his father and his ancestors—scholars, theologians, and jurists. Until the age of thirty-seven he seems to have been a conventional teacher under the royal patronage. In 1244 he met the wandering dervish, Shams of Tabriz. "What I had thought of before as God, I met today in a person." This recognition strengthened and galvanized his belief. His poetry filled with a longing to be the Friend, the close spiritual presence he first saw in Shams, later in Saladin Zarkub, the goldsmith, still later in his scribe, Husam. Rumi died December 17, 1273. During the last thirty years of his life he became a brilliant unfolding of that recognition, and a cause of its incandescence in others.

Pronouns

In Rumi's poetry there is always the mystery of the pronouns. Who is this *you* he addresses? Shams? Saladin Zarkub? Husam? The inner, angelic counterpart? The divine Beloved? A God-Person alloyed of the longing of lover for Beloved? The Friend? All the above? Pronouns dissolve within the pressure of Rumi's recognition of his true identity. The essential power of Rumi's poetry is ecstasy, an ecstasy melting the confinement of the ego into a larger, elastic, cross-pollinating dance of Selves. His is not the ecstasy of Union, not in the poetry. It is a love-ecstasy mixed with some brokenness and much longing. So the pronouns are problematic. Rumi is speaking of a fluctuating exchange between beings, and between beings and Being. Pronouns, particularly in English, cannot record this process. They refer either to oneself or to others, not to the mixing. Rumi's Persian has the all purpose *u* (he, she, it, God), but still the difficulty exists. Even the first person pronouns (*I, me, we, us*) may refer to an impersonal self—a self that according to Sufi doctrine can lose itself in the nothingness of annihilation in God. Many of Rumi's odes end with a disclaimer, sometimes an apology, that words are deceptive, even dangerously abstracted and conceptual. No pronoun can speak the reality he experiences. There must remain a splendid mystery in the presence/s of Rumi's poems. It is the secret recognition (*We have ways within each other that will never be said by anyone.*) of friend and Friend, Rumi and Shams, actual personality and divine being, coordinate identities between and among. These poems are spontaneous voices from the pieces. Rumi is being torn apart by the dizzying reality he is encountering in the odes and quatrains. It is not quite accurate to think of these as "teaching" poems, as perhaps the *Mathnawi* should be. Rumi's odes are not roadmaps for the spiritual path, not directional as perhaps are Han-Shan's poems, for instance. (In Gary Snyder's translation, "Try to make it to Cold Mountain.") Rumi's odes and quatrains rather are the personal, human records of a man's being given a sharp, clear consciousness of the divine, and enduring it.

Chip Buddhas

What of the incredible numbers on these poems? They refer to the Furuzanfar edition of Rumi's work (Tehran), and they indicate a related mystery in Rumi's work, the spontaneous proliferation. The generosity of all these words reminds one of the devotion of the 17th Century Zen monk, Enku, who wanted to carve 120,000 Buddhas in his lifetime, and did. He never wasted a scrap of wood. Presented with an enormous block of cypress and asked to carve two guardian figures for a temple gate, he soon completed those with his hatchet and went on, carving thousands of large and small Buddhas, some no bigger than a finger, from the leftover pieces. *Koppa-butsu*, "chip Buddhas," they became known as. Rumi spins and gives away his language with Enku's fine, intuitive joy. Enku once went up to a raftsman who had tied up his raft on the riverbank, asking for some wood to carve Buddha figures to dedicate to the river. "Certainly, you can take the whole raft if you want." The next morning the raftsman couldn't find his raft. He went to the temple and asked. "Oh, I accepted your kind offer. I carved a thousand images and floated them down the river." The number 3438 over a long ode is as dumbfounding to a reader as the missing raft. The river of Rumi's enthusiasm flows with such relentless variety.

The Restlessness

Jacob Boehme says, "Whatever the self describes, describes the self." These Rumi poems *are* what they describe, a dimension of mystical consciousness where continual dying-birthing occurs. *I leapt from you and you devoured me* (#2399). In the fluidity of his searching Rumi keeps seeing charisma around him, particularly in people, absorbing that, dissolving the image, re-forming, embodying and dissolving again. The poems move, scattering and gathering, evolving. They seem to dilate through stages.

> God's joy moves from unmarked box to unmarked box,
> from cell to cell. As rainwater, down into flowerbed.
> As roses, up from ground.
> Now it looks like a plate of rice and fish,
> now a cliff covered with vines,
> now a horse being saddled.
> It hides within these,
> till one day it cracks them open. (1937)

They move in and out of passionate knowing.

> There's the light of gold of wheat in the sun
> and the gold of bread made from that wheat.
> I have neither. I'm only talking about them. (1937)

They often face the paradox of being caught in between, *not being here and being completely here.* The poems act as midwives to their own next form. They long to die into a glance that ransacks the house of the self,

> . . . so that no one lives here anymore,
> just a boy running barefooted all through it.

The longing is for transformation that causes further transformation, as when an arrow becomes bow and bowstring (2465), intention becomes a source of intention, forgetfulness becomes instruction on how to pray.

The restless changing is a sign of health, fieriness, fermenting, and magnetic movement, all indications of love's action.

> If the sun were not in love, he would have no brightness, . . .
> The ocean would come to rest somewhere. (2674)

Shams himself described Rumi as "ever-changing, always revealing a quality that hadn't been there before!" Rumi composes, with melting terms, a fluctuating music of presence and absence. His work becomes the clear, watery medium for a condition of incarnation: Occasional ecstasy, continuous wonderment and longing, disconnections, union.

> When one is united to the core of another, to speak of that
> is to breathe the name *Hu*, empty of self,
> filled with love.

(*Mathnawi*, Book VI, 4044–5)

C. B.
J. M.

The Oldest Love in New Shapes

Intricate sounds, not words. I catch
what I can't quite make out. Fire burning down
along the roots, as well as in the branches.
The whole tree gone.

Stories about the Green Man Khidr, and stories
Khidr himself told come back. We thought they were lost.

The oldest love in new shapes.
For the sun we say, and the sun comes out.
Lam Yakon, we begin reading Sura 112:
There is no way to compare God to anything.
And look!

I. Quatrains

12

Late, by myself, in the boat of myself,
no light and no land anywhere,
cloudcover thick. I try to stay
just above the surface, yet I'm already under
and living within the ocean.

17

I'm crying, my tears tell me that much.
Last Spring, they say, *the new green, how weak you felt.*

Remember any night of all our nights,
but don't remember things I've said.

25

Friend, our closeness is this:
Anywhere you put your foot, feel me
in the firmness under you.

How is it with this love,
I see your world and not you?

36

When I am with you, we stay up all night.
When you're not here, I can't go to sleep.

Praise God for these two insomnias!
And the difference between them.

64

When I die, lay out the corpse.
You may want to kiss my lips,
just beginning to decay. Don't be frightened
if I open my eyes.

65

This bleating eventually stops. The wolf appears.
We run off in different directions,
with always some thought of how lucky we are.

But nothing floats for long.
Death floods in the mouth and the ear.
Every head goes under and away.

77

For years, copying other people, I tried to know myself.
From within, I couldn't decide what to do.
Unable to see, I heard my name being called.
Then I walked outside.

82

Today, like every other day, we wake up empty
and frightened. Don't open the door to the study
and begin reading. Take down a musical instrument.

Let the beauty we love be what we do.
There are hundreds of ways to kneel and kiss the ground.

91

The breeze at dawn has secrets to tell you.
                    Don't go back to sleep.
You must ask for what you really want.
                    Don't go back to sleep.
People are going back and forth across the doorsill
                    where the two worlds touch.
The door is round and open.
                    Don't go back to sleep.

116

Take someone who doesn't keep score,
who's not looking to be richer, or afraid of losing,
who has not the slightest interest even
in his own personality: He's free.

158

Out beyond ideas of wrongdoing and rightdoing,
there is a field. I'll meet you there.

When the soul lies down in that grass,
the world is too full to talk about.
Ideas, language, even the phrase *each other*
doesn't make any sense.

388

I would love to kiss you.
The price of kissing is your life.

Now my loving is running toward my life shouting,
What a bargain, let's buy it.

403

We have this way of talking, and we have another.
Apart from what we wish and what we fear may happen,
we are alive with other life, as clear stones
take form in the mountain.

494

Someone who goes with half a loaf of bread
to a small place that fits like a nest around him,
someone who wants no more, who's not himself
longed for by anyone else,

He is a letter to everyone. You open it.
It says, *Live.*

497

Who sees inside from outside?
Who finds hundreds of mysteries
even where minds are deranged?

See through his eyes what he sees.
Who then is looking out from his eyes?

511

The clear bead at the center changes everything.
There are no edges to my loving now.

I've heard it said there's a window that opens
from one mind to another,

but if there's no wall, there's no need
for fitting the window, or the latch.

549

We take long trips.
We puzzle over the meaning of a painting or a book,
when what we're wanting to see and understand
in this world, we *are* that.

551

Does sunset sometimes look like the sun's coming up?
Do you know what a faithful love is like?
You're crying. You say you've burned yourself.
But can you think of anyone who's not
hazy with smoke?

556

Daylight, full of small dancing particles
and the one great turning, our souls
are dancing with you, without feet, they dance.
Can you see them when I whisper in your ear?

558

They try to say what you are, spiritual or sexual?
They wonder about Solomon and all his wives.

In the body of the world, they say, there is a Soul
and you are *that.*

But we have ways within each other
that will never be said by anyone.

568

The human shape is a ghost
made of distraction and pain.
Sometimes pure light, sometimes cruel,
trying wildly to open,
this image tightly held within itself.

11

630

Stay in the company of lovers.
Those other kinds of people, they each
want to show you something.

A crow will lead you to an empty barn,
a parrot to sugar.

667

There is a light seed grain inside.
You fill it with yourself, or it dies.

I'm caught in this curling energy! Your hair!
Whoever's calm and sensible is insane!

670

Don't think of good advice for me.
I've tasted the worst that can happen.
So they lock me somewhere, bound and gagged,
they can't tie up this new love I have.

674

You don't have "bad" days and "good" days.
You don't sometimes feel brilliant and sometimes dumb.
There's no studying, no scholarly thinking having to do with love,
but there is a great deal of plotting, and secret touching,
and nights you can't remember at all.

686

The sufi opens his hands to the universe
and gives away each instant, free.
Unlike someone who begs on the street for money to survive,
a dervish begs to give you his life.

747

There's a strange frenzy in my head,
of birds flying,
each particle circulating on its own.
Is the one I love *every*where?

802

They say that Paradise will be perfect
with lots of clear white wine and all the beautiful women.
We hold on to times like this then,
since this is how it's going to be.

914

Come to the orchard in Spring.
There is light and wine, and sweethearts in the pomegranate
    flowers.
If you do not come, these do not matter.
If you do come, these do not matter.

921

Poles apart, I'm the color of dying, you're the color
of being born. Unless we breathe in each other,
there can be no garden.

So, that's why plants grow and laugh at our eyes,
which focus on distance.

14

1078

Think that you're gliding out from the face of a cliff
like an eagle. Think you're walking
like a tiger walks by himself in the forest.
You're most handsome when you're after food.

Spend less time with nightingales and peacocks.
One is just a voice, the other just a color.

1082

For a while we lived with people,
but we saw no sign in them of the faithfulness we wanted.
It's better to hide completely within
as water hides in metal, as fire hides in a rock.

1088

The mystery does not get clearer by repeating the question,
nor is it bought with going to amazing places.

Until you've kept your eyes
and your wanting still for fifty years,
you don't begin to cross over from confusion.

1115

The minute I'm disappointed, I feel encouraged.
When I'm ruined, I'm healed.
When I'm quiet and solid as the ground, then I talk
the low tones of thunder for everyone.

1127

I drink streamwater and the air
becomes clearer and everything I do.

I become a waterwheel,
turning and tasting you, as long
as water moves.

1131

In pain, I breathe easier.
The scared child is running from the house, screaming.
I hear the gentleness.

Under nine layers of illusion, whatever the light,
on the face of any object, in the ground itself,
I see your face.

16

1146

Today I'm out wandering, turning my skull
into a cup for others to drink wine from.
In this town somewhere there sits a calm, intelligent man,
who doesn't know what he's about to do!

1193

I asked for one kiss: You gave me six.
Who was teacher is now student.
Things good and generous take form
in me, and the air is clear.

1238

I am insane, but they keep calling to me.
No one here knows me, but no one chases me off.
My job is to stay awake like the nightwatchman.
When they're drunk enough, and it's late enough,
they recognize me. They say, *There's daylight.*

1242

During the day I was singing with you.
At night we slept in the same bed.
I wasn't conscious day or night.
I thought I knew who I was,
but I was you.

1243

Drinking wine with you, getting warmer and warmer,
I think why not trade in this overcoat
made of leaves and dirt.
Then I look out the window.
For what? Both worlds are here.

1245

Since we've seen each other, a game goes on.
Secretly I move, and you respond.
You're winning, you think it's funny.

But look up from the board now, look how
I've brought in furniture to this invisible place,
so we can live here.

1246

The minute I heard my first love story
I started looking for you, not knowing'
how blind that was.

Lovers don't finally meet somewhere.
They're in each other all along.

1287

If you have any patience left, we know what to do.
If you love sleep, we'll tear you away.
If you change into a mountain, we'll melt you.
If you become an ocean, we'll drain you.

1300

You say you have no sexual longing any more.
You're one with the one you love.

This is dangerous.
Don't believe that I have a love like that.

If one day you see a picture of how you think,
you'll hate yourself, openly.

1303

I'm not talking out loud. I'm talking
to the ears of your spirit.
Remember what I've said. Tomorrow
I'll say openly what I'm saying tonight.

1315

We've given up making a living.
It's all this crazy love poetry now.

It's everywhere. Our eyes and our feelings
focus together, with our words.

1319

We have a huge barrel of wine, but no cups.
That's fine with us. Every morning
we glow and in the evening we glow again.

They say there's no future for us. They're right.
Which is fine with us.

1359

Do you think I know what I'm doing?
That for one breath or half-breath I belong to myself?
As much as a pen knows what it's writing,
or the ball can guess where it's going next.

1504

Do not sit long with a sad friend.
When you go to a garden,
do you look at thorns or flowers?
Spend more time with roses and jasmine.

1616

Inside the Great Mystery that is,
we don't really own anything.
What is this competition we feel then,
before we go, one at a time, through the same gate?

1652

We are the mirror as well as the face in it.
We are tasting the taste this minute
of eternity. We are pain
and what cures pain. We are
the sweet, cold water and the jar that pours.

1794

At night we fall into each other with such grace.
When it's light, you throw me back
like you do your hair.

Your eyes now drunk with God,
mine with looking at you,
one drunkard takes care of another.

1797

We are walking through a garden.
I turn away for a minute.
You're doing it again.
You have my face here, but you look at flowers!

II. Odes

7

Now That I Know How It Is

I'm here by the gate.
Maybe you'll throw open a door and call.
I'm drenched with being here,
rambling drunk. Things dissolve around me,
but I'm still sitting here.

One clap in the emptiness of space. New centuries begin.
Laughter. A rose, a wise loveliness, the sun
coming out brilliantly, on horseback.
All this day we'll be close, drinking and joking,
close to your face. Whenever I say *your face*,
my soul jumps out of its skin!

Is there some other roof somewhere? Any name
other than yours? Any glass of wine other than this
you bring me so perfectly?
If I find my life, I'll never let go,
holding and twisting the cloth of your coat
as in that dream when I saw you.

By this gate kings are waiting with me.
Your eyes, I'm lost remembering your eyes.
Look at us out here moaning with our shirts ripped open.
Anyone seeing your face and not obsessed with the sight
is cold as a rock in the ground.
What further curse could I put on him?

What's worse than having no word from you?
Don't waste your life with those who don't see you.
Stay with us. We're each running across the beach,
torn loose from friends, making friends with the sea.
One flood moves in its sleep. One's confused
out of its channel. One says *All praise to God.*
Another, *No strength but yours.*

You are sunlight come as wagonloads of presents
and free wine for the poor.
A rose looks up and the calyx rips open.
The lute player with quick fingers sees your hands
and stops and closes her eyes.

Who is luckiest in this whole orchestra? The reed.
Its mouth touches your lips to learn music.
All reeds, sugarcane especially, think only
of this chance. They sway in the canebrakes,
free in the many ways they dance.

Without you the instruments would die.
One sits close beside you. Another takes a long kiss.
The tambourine begs, *Touch my skin so I can be myself.*
Let me feel you enter each limb bone by bone,
that what died last night can be whole today.

Why live some soberer way and feel you ebbing out?
I won't do it.
Either give me enough wine or leave me alone,
now that I know how it is
to be with you in a constant conversation.

There's Nothing Ahead

Lovers think they're looking for each other,
but there's only one search: Wandering
this world is wandering that, both inside one
transparent sky. In here
there is no dogma and no heresy.

The miracle of Jesus is himself, not what he said or did
about the future. Forget the future.
I'd worship someone who could do that!

On the way you may want to look back, or not,
but if you can say *There's nothing ahead,*
there will be nothing there.

Stretch your arms and take hold the cloth of your clothes
with both hands. The cure for pain is in the pain.
Good and bad are mixed. If you don't have both,
you don't belong with us.

When one of us gets lost, is not here, he must be inside us.
There's no place like that anywhere in the world.

Someone Digging in the Ground

An eye is meant to see things.
The soul is here for its own joy.
A head has one use: For loving a true love.
Legs: To run after.

Love is for vanishing into the sky. The mind,
for learning what men have done and tried to do.
Mysteries are not to be solved. The eye goes blind
when it only wants to see *why*.

A lover is always accused of something.
But when he finds his love, whatever was lost
in the looking comes back completely changed.
On the way to Mecca, many dangers: Thieves,
the blowing sand, only camel's milk to drink.
Still, each pilgrim kisses the black stone there
with pure longing, feeling in the surface
the taste of the lips he wants.

This talk is like stamping new coins. They pile up,
while the real work is done outside
by someone digging in the ground.

Walking Out of the Treasury Building

Lord, the air smells good today, straight from the mysteries
within the inner courts of God.
A grace like new clothes thrown
across the garden, free medicine for everybody.
The trees in their prayer, the birds in praise,
the first blue violets kneeling.
Whatever came from Being is caught up in being, drunkenly
forgetting the way back.

One man turns and sees his birth
pulling separate from the others.
He fills with light, and colors change here.
He drinks it in, and everyone is wonderfully
drunk, shining with his beauty.
I can't really say that I feel the pain of others,
when the whole world seems so sweet.

Face to face with a lion, I grow leonine.
Walking out of the Treasury Building, I feel generous.
Anyone still sober in this weather must be afraid
of people, afraid what they'll say.
Enough talking. If we eat too much greenery,
we're going to smell like vegetables.

The Elusive Ones

They're lovers again: Sugar dissolving in milk.
Day and night, no difference. The sun *is* the moon:
An amalgam. Their gold and silver melt together.
This is the season when the dead branch and the green
branch are the same branch.

The cynic bites his finger because he can't understand.
Omar and Ali on the same throne, two kings in one belt.
Nightmares fill with light like a holiday.
Men and angels speak one language.
The elusive ones finally meet.

The essence and the evolving forms
run to meet each other like children
to their father and mother.
Good and evil, dead and alive, everything blooms
from one natural stem.

You know this already, I'll stop.
Any direction you turn it's one vision.
Shams, my body is a candle touched with fire.

This World Which Is Made of Our Love for Emptiness

Praise to the emptiness that blanks out existence. Existence:
This place made from our love for that emptiness!
Yet somehow comes emptiness,
this existence goes.
Praise to that happening, over and over!

For years I pulled my own existence out of emptiness.
Then one swoop, one swing of the arm,
that work is over.
Free of who I was, free of presence, free of
dangerous fear, hope,
free of mountainous wanting.
The here-and-now mountain is a tiny piece of a piece
of straw
blown off into emptiness.

These words I'm saying so much begin to lose meaning:
Existence, emptiness, mountain, straw:
Words and what they try to say swept
out the window, down the slant of the roof.

Maybe They're Shy

Now the nightbirds will be singing
of the way we love each other.
Why should they sing about flowers
when they've seen us in the garden?

Maybe they're shy. They can't look at the face,
so they describe feet.
If they keep dividing love into pieces,
they'll disappear altogether. We must be gentle
and explain it to them.

Think of a mountain so huge the Caucasus Range
is a tiny speck. Normal mountains
run toward her when she calls.
They listen in their cave-ears and echo back.
They turn upsidedown when they get close,
they're so excited.

No more words. In the name of this place we drink in
with our breathing, stay quiet like a flower.
So the nightbirds will start singing.

Champion Lovemaker and Leader of Men.

If you could not feel tenderness and hurt.
If you could live in the poorhouse of not-wanting
and never be indignant.
If you could take two steps away from the beautiful one
you want so much to lie down with.
If you could trust there's a spirit-wife
for you somewhere, a whole harem of wives,
a nest, a jewel-setting where
when you sit down, you know
you've always wanted to be.
If you could quit living here and go there.
If you could remember clearly what you've done.

But strong hooks hold you in this wind.
So many people love you,
you mix with the color and smell and taste of surroundings.
Champion lovemaker and leader of men!
You can't give up your public fascination,
or your compassion for the dying.

There's another compassion you don't know yet,
but you may, when griefs disappear.
It's a place,
with no questioning thorns in the pasture grass.
If you could remember you're not a crow,
but the mystic osprey that never needs to light,
you could be walking there
with Shams.

The Tent

Outside, the freezing desert night.
This other night inside grows warm, kindling.
Let the landscape be covered with thorny crust.
We have a soft garden in here.
The continents blasted,
cities and little towns, everything
become a scorched, blackened ball.

The news we hear is full of grief for that future,
but the real news inside here
is there's no news at all.

Greed and Generosity

Look at her face.
Open your eyes into her eyes.
When she laughs, everyone falls in love.
Lift your head up off the table. See,
there are no edges to this garden.
Sweet fruits, every kind you can think of,
branches green and always
slightly moving.

How long should you look at earth's face?
Come back and look again.
Now you see the nervous greed
deep inside plants and animals. Now you see them
constantly giving themselves away.

Greed and generosity are evidence of love.
If you can't see love itself,
see the results.
If you can't find love-colors in anything,
look for the pale, tired face of a lover.

Take this town with its stores and everyone
rushing around, some with a lot of money,
some without any.

The Whole Place Goes Up

Today with Spring here finally we ought to be living
outdoors with our friends.
Let's go to those strangers in the field
and dance around them like bees from flower to flower,
building in the beehive air
our true hexagonal homes.

Someone comes in from outside saying,
Don't play music just for yourselves.
Now we're tearing up the house like a drum,
collapsing walls with our pounding.
We hear a voice from the sky calling the lovers
and the odd, lost people. We scatter lives.
We break what holds us, each one a blacksmith
heating iron and walking to the anvil.
We blow on the inner fire.
With each striking we change.

The whole place goes up, all stability gone to smoke.
Sometimes high, sometimes low, we begin anywhere,
we have no method.
We're the bat swung by powerful arms.
Balls keep rolling from us, thousands of them underfoot.

Now we're still. Silence also is wisdom, a flame
hiding in cotton wool.

Who Says Words With My Mouth

All day I think about it, then.at night I say it.
Where did I come from, and what am I supposed to be doing?
I have no idea.
My soul is from elsewhere, I'm sure of that,
and I intend to end up there.

This drunkenness began in some other tavern.
When I get back around to that place,
I'll be completely sober. Meanwhile,
I'm like a bird from another continent, sitting in this aviary.
The day is coming when I fly off,
but who is it now in my ear, who hears my voice?
Who says words with my mouth?

Who looks out with my eyes? What is the soul?
I cannot stop asking.
If I could taste one sip of an answer,
I could break out of this prison for drunks.
I didn't come here of my own accord, and I can't leave that way.
Whoever brought me here will have to take me back.

This poetry. I never know what I'm going to say.
I don't plan it.
When I'm outside the saying of it,
I get very quiet and rarely speak at all.

(From the Safa Anthology)

III. Versions Done from the Translations of Arberry and Nicholson

Answers from the Elements

A whole afternoon field inside me from one stem of reed.
The messenger comes running toward me, irritated:
Why be so hard to find?

Last night I asked the moon about the Moon, my one question
for the visible world, Where is God?
The moon says, *I am dust stirred up
when he passed by.* The sun, *My face is pale yellow
from just now seeing him.* Water: *I slide on my head and face
like a snake, from a spell he said.* Fire: *His lightning,
I want to be that restless.* Wind, why so light?
I would burn if I had a choice. Earth, quiet
and thoughtful? *Inside me I have a garden
and an underground spring.*

This world hurts my head with its answers,
wine filling my hand, not my glass.
If I could wake completely, I would say without speaking
why I'm ashamed of using words.

Fasting

There's hidden sweetness in the stomach's emptiness.
We are lutes, no more, no less. If the soundbox
is stuffed full of anything, no music.
If the brain and the belly are burning clean
with fasting, every moment a new song comes out of the fire.
The fog clears, and new energy makes you
run up the steps in front of you.
Be emptier and cry like reed instruments cry.
Emptier, write secrets with the reed pen.
When you're full of food and drink, Satan sits
where your spirit should, an ugly metal statue
in place of the Kaaba. When you fast,
good habits gather like friends who want to help.
Fasting is Solomon's ring. Don't give it
to some illusion and lose your power,
but even if you have, if you've lost all will and control,
they come back when you fast, like soldiers appearing
out of the ground, pennants flying above them.
A table descends to your tents,
Jesus' table.
Expect to see it, when you fast, this table
spread with other food, better than the broth of cabbages.

An Egypt That Doesn't Exist

I want to say words that flame
as I say them, but I keep quiet and don't try
to make both worlds fit in one mouthful.

I keep secret in myself an Egypt
that doesn't exist.
Is that good or bad? I don't know.

For years I gave away sexual love
with my eyes. Now I don't.
I'm not in any one place. I don't have a name
for what I give away. Whatever Shams
gave, that you can have from me.

1850

Growing a Coat of Mail

Light going dim. Is it my eyes, or a cloud, or the sun
itself, or the window? I can't see the point
of the needle, or the other end of the thread.

I want that moment again when I spread out
like olive oil in the skillet.
The same heat makes iron steel. Abraham,
a bed of jasmine sitting quietly, or talking.

Unmanned, I'm a true person,
or at least the ring knocker on the door where they live.
The Prophet says, *Fasting protects.* Do that.
On dry land a fish needs to be wrapped in something.
In the ocean, as you see, it grows a coat of mail.

The New Rule

It's the old rule that drunks have to argue
and get into fights.
The lover is just as bad: He falls into a hole.
But down in that hole he finds something shining,
worth more than any amount of money or power.

Last night the moon came dropping its clothes in the street.
I took it as a sign to start singing,
falling *up* into the bowl of sky.
The bowl breaks. Everywhere is falling everywhere.
Nothing else to do.

Here's the new rule: Break the wineglass,
and fall toward the glassblower's breath.

Unmarked Boxes

Don't grieve. Anything you lose comes round
in another form. The child weaned from mother's milk
now drinks wine and honey mixed.

God's joy moves from unmarked box to unmarked box,
from cell to cell. As rainwater, down into flowerbed.
As roses, up from ground.
Now it looks like a plate of rice and fish,
now a cliff covered with vines,
now a horse being saddled.
It hides within these,
till one day it cracks them open.

Part of the self leaves the body when we sleep
and changes shape. You might say, "Last night
I was a cypress tree, a small bed of tulips,
a field of grapevines." Then the phantasm goes away.
You're back in the room.
I don't want to make any one fearful.
Hear what's behind what I say.

Tatatumtum tatum tatadum.
There's the light gold of wheat in the sun
and the gold of bread made from that wheat.
I have neither. I'm only talking about them,

as a town in the desert looks up
at stars on a clear night.

2015

I Have Such a Teacher

Last night my teacher taught me the lesson of Poverty:
Having nothing and wanting nothing.

I am a naked man standing inside a mine of rubies,
clothed in red silk.
I absorb the shining and now I see the ocean,
billions of simultaneous motions
moving in me.
A circle of lovely, quiet people
becomes the ring on my finger.

Then the wind and thunder of rain on the way.
I have such a teacher.

Bonfire at Midnight

A shout comes out of my room
where I've been cooped up.
After all my lust and dead living I can still live with you.
You want me to.
You fix and bring me food.
You forget the way I've been.

The ocean moves and surges in the heat
of the middle of the day,
in the heat of this thought I'm having.
Why aren't all human resistances burning up with this thought?

It's a drum and arms waving.
It's a bonfire at midnight on the top edge of a hill,
this meeting again with you.

The Bottle Is Corked

The rock splits open like wings beat
air, wanting. Campfire gives in to rain,
but I can't go to sleep, or be patient.

Part of me wants to eat the stones
and hold you back when you're leaving,
till your good laughing turns bitter and wrong.

I worry I won't have someone to talk to, and breathe with.
Don't you understand I'm some kind of food for you?
I'm a place where you can work.

The bottle is corked and sitting on the table.
Someone comes in and sees me without you
and puts his hand on my head like I'm a child.
This is so difficult.

Be Melting Snow

Totally conscious, and apropos of nothing, you come to see me.
Is someone here? I ask.
The moon. The full moon is inside your house.

My friends and I go running out into the street.
I'm in here, comes a voice from the house, but we aren't listening.
We're looking up at the sky.
My pet nightingale sobs like a drunk in the garden.
Ringdoves scatter with small cries, *Where, Where.*
It's midnight. The whole neighborhood is up and out in the street
thinking, *The cat-burglar has come back.*
The actual thief is there too, saying out loud,
Yes, the cat-burglar is somewhere in this crowd.
No one pays attention.

Lo, I am with you always, means when you look for God,
God is in the look of your eyes,
in the thought of looking, nearer to you than your self,
or things that have happened to you.
There's no need to go outside.
Be melting snow.
Wash yourself of yourself.

A white flower grows in the quietness.
Let your tongue become that flower.

The Image of Your Body

You've made it out of the city,
that image of your body, trembling with traffic
and fear slips behind.
Your face arrives in the redbud trees, and the tulips.

You're still restless.
Climb up the ladder to the roof.
You're by yourself a lot,
become the one that when you walk in,
luck shifts to the one who needs it.
If you've not been fed, be bread.

In the Arc of Your Mallet

Don't go anywhere without me.
Let nothing happen in the sky apart from me,
or on the ground, in this world or that world,
without my being in its happening.
Vision, see nothing I don't see.
Language, say nothing.
The way the night knows itself with the moon,
be that with me. Be the rose
nearest to the thorn that I am.
I want to feel myself in you when you taste food, in the arc
of your mallet when you work.
When you visit friends, when you go
up on the roof by yourself at night.

There's nothing worse than to walk out along the street
without you. I don't know where I'm going.
You're the road and the knower of roads,
more than maps, more than love.

The Ocean Moving All Night

Stay with us. Don't sink to the bottom
like a fish going to sleep.
Be with the ocean moving steadily all night,
not scattered like a rainstorm.

The spring we're looking for
is somewhere in this murkiness.
See the night-lights up there traveling together,
the candle awake in its gold dish.

Don't slide into the cracks of ground like spilled mercury.
When the full moon comes out, look around.

Folded Into the River

Your face is the light in here that makes
my arms full of gentleness.
The beginning of a month-long holiday, the disc
of the full moon, the shade of your hair,
these draw me in. I dive
into the deep pool of a mountain river,
folded into union,
as the split-second when the bat meets the ball,
and there is one cry between us.

Let's Go Home

Late and starting to rain, it's time to go home.
We've wandered long enough in empty buildings.
I know it's tempting to stay and meet those new people.
I know it's even more sensible
to spend the night here with them,
but I want to be home.

We've seen enough beautiful places with signs on them
saying *This Is God's House.*
That's seeing the grain like the ants do,
without the work of harvesting.
Let's leave grazing to cows and go
where we know what everyone really intends,
where we can walk around without clothes on.

Privacy

Who is this standing in my house? He signals with his hand,
What do you want from me? Nourishment,
and the privacy of one truth.

There are so many deceptive people pretending
to be faithful. Don't sit among them, eyes shut
like a bud, mouth open like a rose.

The world is a mirror, an imaging of Love's perfection.
No man has ever seen a part greater than the whole.
Go on foot through this garden like the grass does.
Only the rose is riding, all the rest on foot.
Rose, both sword and swordsman,
Reason in the abstract, and reasoning in each of us.

Generous Saladin, let your hand be
a constant necklace on my neck.

The Drunk and the Madman

I'm lost in your face, in your lost eyes.
The drunk and the madman inside me
take a liking to each other. They sit down
on the ground together. Look at this mess
of a life as the sun looks fondly into ruins.

With one glance many trees grow from a single seed.
Your two eyes are like a Turk born in Persia.
He's on a rampage, a Persian shooting Turkish arrows.
He has ransacked my house so that no one lives here anymore,
just a boy running barefooted all through it.

Your face is a garden that comes up where the house was.
With our hands we tear down houses and make bare places.
The moon has no desire to be described.
No one *needs* this poetry.
The loose hair-strands of a beautiful woman
don't *have* to be combed.

Silver Coins

Put your cheek against this drunken cheek.
Forget anger and men planning war.
When I hold out silver coins, take them, and give
me a cup of liquid full of gold light.
You can open the wide door of the sky.
Surely you will open me. All I have
is this emptiness. Give it a nickname.
Breaker and healer, break and heal this head.
Don't press your seal to that pistachio nut.
Put it here. There is that in me
that has to be told fifty times a day:
Stop hunting. Step on this net.

Keeper of Secrets

You came here to tell my secret to everyone, what I give
no sign of. Last night in a dream you offered
a cup. I said, I will not drink wine,
Do not, the loss is yours.
I'm afraid of being shamed. I'll reach for you
and you won't be there. *It's astonishing to me*
that someone offers you his innermost life, and you frown.
Would you be deceptive with me as you do with others?
I am the Keeper of Secrets. You can't hide from me.
I am the beauty of the perceived world, but you lay back
on the ground. I am the true direction of the spirit,
but you glance around at clouds.

Look here. If you angrily turn away now,
you will do the same on the day you die. Be pale
for the One who created color. Don't put saffron
on your face for the sake of shadows.
Be a rooster, conscious of time and the leader.
Don't change your rooster to a hen.
Bend and sit crookedly, but tell the straight truth.
Truth is enough. I am the Friend, your spirit.
Why look for someone else?

If you like the verse about lending to God, lend a clipping
from a counterfeit coin and get back the deed to a diamond mine.
If for two or three days you bandage your eyes with awe,
you make your sensible eyes a fountain for the other ocean.
If for only a second you go straight for this target,
that arrowy intention becomes your bow and bowstring.
There's no generosity better than this: That with your sins
and forgetfulness I'm telling you how to pray.

So much for words which have to be written down,
or not contained in the mouth. If you were to open
every living particle, you could make a mouth of each.

Look, Fish

I saw the Friend clearly, and I stopped reading
books and memorizing poems.
I quit going to church, and I quit fasting
to be a better person.
I quit worrying about when I should be praying.
I saw how I was undisciplined and toxic.
I saw how lovely and strong.
No mercy for the drunk, a full sentence!

Let the beautiful one come out in fine clothes.
Wind his hair into God's rope. Twist the braids
into a cross for Christians to see.
His light is better than the sun's. How could he
have gotten so withered and weak?
Now he jokes and pounds the table. He was
wine under a lid, Joseph at the bottom of the well.
Know yourself in the light of the true ones,
as the ground sees its face in a garden,
as rock knows its own secret
put next to a ruby, iron
next to polished steel. Come into existence.

Flies go round to every pile of dung and finally
out of that compost the Anya bird, the true man.
When a person is born of this new moment,
it does not wear off tomorrow.
Sit with lovers and be useful. Don't wander away.
Look, fish, at the ocean behind you.
Go back where you came from, sea creature.

You hear the sound of water and you know where you want to be.
Why wait? You've gone places you regret going,
for money and such. Don't do that again.
Water says, *Live here.*
Don't carry me around in buckets and pans.
False duties! Rest and be quiet.

Let the Letter Read You

Why stay so long where your words are scattered
and doing no good? I've sent a letter a day
for a hundred days. Either you don't read the mail,
or you've forgotten how to leave.

Let the letter read you. Come back.
No one understands who you are in that prison
for the stonefaced. You've escaped,
but still you sit there like a falcon
on the window ledge. You are both water
and stream, but you think you need something
to drink like a lion or a deer.

How far is it? How far is the light of the moon
from the moon? How far is the taste of candy
from the lip? Every second you give away light.
We accept. We like this market.

Your love is a sweet poison we eat from your hand
to dissolve and drain away the ego-life
now spraying this fountain from us.

Sometimes I Forget Completely

Sometimes I forget completely
what companionship is.
Unconscious and insane, I spill sad
energy everywhere. My story
gets told in various ways: A romance,
a dirty joke, a war, a vacancy.

Divide up my forgetfulness to any number,
it will go around.
These dark suggestions that I follow,
are they part of some plan?
Friends, be careful. Don't come near me
out of curiosity, or sympathy.

2558

The Rights of Crying

Why so fugitive? I have some right
to be with you, rights of crying.

If there were laughter all around me,
I would feel closed in if you weren't there.
With my children and everyone else I love,
I'd still be distracted.

How can I tie down one of your feet?
I do have enough strength and patience.
No matter how far you go, even
beyond sunlight into where Jesus is visible,
I'll come and wait to be told
why you go away from me.

After Being in Love, the Next Responsibility

Turn me like a waterwheel turning a millstone.
Plenty of water, a Living River.
Keep me in one place and scatter the love.
Leaf-moves in wind, straw drawn toward amber,
all parts of the world are in love,
but they do not tell their secrets: Cows grazing
on a sacramental table, ants whispering in Solomon's ear.
Mountains mumbling an echo. Sky, calm.
If the sun were not in love, he would have no brightness,
the side of the hill no grass on it.
The ocean would come to rest somewhere.

Be a lover as they are, that you come to know
your Beloved. Be faithful that you may know
Faith. The other parts of the universe did not accept
the next responsibility of love as you can.
They were afraid they might make a mistake
with it, the inspired knowing
that springs from being in love.

The Diver's Clothes Lying Empty

You're sitting here with us, but you're also out walking
in a field at dawn. You are yourself
the animal we hunt when you come with us on the hunt.
You're in your body like a plant is solid in the ground,
yet you're wind. You're the diver's clothes
lying empty on the beach. You're the fish.

In the ocean are many bright strands
and many dark strands like veins that are seen
when a wing is lifted up.
Your hidden self is blood in those, those veins
that are lute strings that make ocean music,
not the sad edge of surf, but the sound of no shore.

An Empty Garlic

You miss the garden,
because you want a small fig from a random tree.
You don't meet the beautiful woman.
You're joking with an old crone.
It makes me want to cry how she detains you,
stinking-mouthed, with a hundred talons,
putting her head over the roofedge to call down,
tasteless fig, fold over fold, empty
as dry-rotten garlic.

She has you tight by the belt,
even though there's no flower and no milk
inside her body.
Death will open your eyes
to what her face is: Leather spine
of a black lizard. No more advice.

Let yourself be silently drawn
by the stronger pull of what you really love.

The Shop

Lightning falling on the helpless, a surge of pearl out of the rock,
covering the rock, this life torn into a hundred pieces,
and one of those pieces a ticket
to let me back into my life.

A spirit-world divided into eight sections, one a scroll.
Eight scrolls in the parchment of your face.
What kind of bird am I becoming, kneeling like a camel,
pecking at the fire like an ostrich?

You and I have worked in the same shop for years.
Our loves are great fellow-workers.
Friends cluster there and every moment we notice
a new light coming out in the sky.
Invisible, yet taking form, like Christ coming through
Mary. In the cradle, God.

Shams, why this inconsistency?
That we live within love
and yet we run away?

67

The Torrent Leaves

Rise up nimbly and go on your strange journey
to the ocean of meanings where you become one of those.
From one terrace to another through clay banks,
washing your wings with watery silt,
follow your friends. The pitcher breaks.
You're in the moving river. Living Water,
how long will you make clay pitchers
that have to be broken to enter you?
The torrent knows it can't stay on this mountain.
Leave and don't look away from the Sun as you go.
Through him you are sometimes crescent, sometimes full.

Say Yes Quickly

Forget your life. Say *God is Great*. Get up.
You think you know what time it is. It's time to pray.
You've carved so many little figurines, too many.
Don't knock on any random door like a beggar.
Reach your long hand out to another door, beyond where
you go on the street, the street
where eveyone says, "How are you?"
and no one says *How aren't you?*

Tomorrow you'll see what you've broken and torn tonight,
thrashing in the dark. Inside you
there's an artist you don't know about.
He's not interested in how things look different in moonlight.

If you are here unfaithfully with us,
you're causing terrible damage.
If you've opened your loving to God's love,
you're helping people you don't know
and have never seen.

Is what I say true? Say *yes* quickly,
if you know, if you've known it
from before the beginning of the universe.

Dissolver of Sugar

Dissolver of sugar, dissolve me,
if this is the time.
Do it gently with a touch of a hand, or a look.
Every morning I wait at dawn. That's when it's happened before
Or do it suddenly like an execution. How else
can I get ready for death?

You breathe without a body like a spark.
You grieve, and I begin to feel lighter.
You keep me away with your arm,
but the keeping away is pulling me in.

Strange Business

If you don't have a woman that lives with you,
why aren't you looking?
If you have one, why aren't you satisfied?
You have no resistance to your friend.
Why don't you become the Friend?
If the flute is too quiet to say,
teach it manners.
Someone's holding you back, break off.

You sit here for days saying, *This is strange business.*
You're the strange business.
You have the energy of the sun in you,
but you keep knotting it up at the base of your spine.
You're some weird kind of gold that wants to stay melted
in the furnace, so you won't have to be coins.
Say ONE in your lonesome house.
Loving two is hiding inside your self.

You've gotten drunk on so many kinds of wine.
Taste this. It won't make you wild.
It's fire. Give up,
if you don't understand by this time
that your living is firewood.

This wave of talking builds. Better
we should not speak it, but let it grow within.

The Snow-World Melts

Think of the phoenix coming up out of ashes,
but not flying off.
For a moment we have form.
We can't see.
How can we be conscious and you be conscious
at the same time and separate?
Copper when an alchemist works on it loses its copper
qualities. Seeds in Spring
begin to be trees, no longer seed. Brushwood
put in the fire changes. The snow-world melts.
You step in my footprint and it's gone.

It's not that I've done anything to deserve
this attention from you. Predestination
and freewill: We can argue them,
but they're only ideas. What's real
is a presence, like Shams.

The Name

Do you know a word that doesn't refer to something?
Have you ever picked and held a rose from R,O,S,E?
You say the NAME. Now try to find the reality it names.
Look at the moon in the sky, not the one in the lake.
If you want to be free of your obsession with words
and beautiful lettering, make one stroke down.
There's no self, no characteristics,
but a bright center where you have the knowledge
the Prophets have, without books or interpreter.

(Nicholson, quoted in *Mystics of Islam*, p. 69)

The Music

For sixty years I have been forgetful,
every minute, but not for a second
has this flowing toward me stopped or slowed.
I deserve nothing. Today I recognize
that I am the guest the mystics talk about.
I play this living music for my Host.
Everything today is for the Host.

(Nicholson, *Mathnawi*, Book I, 2084–2085)

Display

There's a kind of person whose expertise
is display, subtly to hold and catch
the eye, builder of lovely traps,
not thinking what constant trap-building does.
You make your friends affectionate for a moment,
then leave. This has been your habit,
now your career, since you were born. Touch
the cloth you've woven of applause and compliments.
Stretch the warp and woof. Is it there?
Your life is more than half gone with you still working
these charming traps. Catch one person,
let another go, no reason for deciding anything,
like children feeling mean, in a game with no rules.
Night. The empty traps follow you back to your house.
You have locked yourself inside disappointment.
No actual hunter would trap himself.
You've seen a man chasing a wild pig. His life is fatigue,
and what he finally gets he can't eat.
Only One is worth chasing with your living.
He can't be trapped. You must throw away your love-traps
and walk into His.

Better be quarry than hunter, a voice says in the air.
Don't try to be the sun. Be a dust mote.
Lunar moth, love the candle.
Taste your life.
Put your shoes on upside down.
Things are reversed from what they should be in this place you
   live now.
One who should be hung on the scaffold is made emperor.
People stand and clap.
Tombs with ornamental plaster, self-conceit everywhere.
Palm trees made of wax, wax leaves and fruit, wax dirt.

(Nicholson, *Mathnawi,* Book V, 395–419)

The Question

One dervish to another, *What was your vision of God's presence?*
I haven't seen anything.
But for the sake of conversation, I'll tell you a story.

God's presence is there in front of me, a fire on the left,
a lovely stream on the right.
One group walks toward the fire, *into* the fire, another
toward the sweet flowing water.
No one knows which are blessed and which not.
Whoever walks into the fire appears suddenly in the stream.
A head goes under on the water surface, that head
pokes out of the fire.
Most people guard against going into the fire,
and so end up in it.
Those who love the water of pleasure and make it their devotion
are cheated with this reversal.
The trickery goes further.
The voice of the fire tells the *truth,* saying *I am not fire.*
I am fountainhead. Come into me and don't mind the sparks.

If you are a friend of God, fire is your water.
You should wish to have a hundred thousand sets of mothwings,
so you could burn them away, one set a night.
The moth sees light and goes into fire. You should see fire
and go toward light. Fire is what of God is world-consuming.
Water, world-protecting.
Somehow each gives the appearance of the other. To these eyes
   you have now
what looks like water burns. What looks like
fire is a great relief to be inside.
You've seen a magician make a bowl of rice
seem a dish full of tiny, live worms.
Before an assembly with one breath he made the floor swarm
with scorpions that weren't there.
How much more amazing God's tricks.
Generation after generation lies down, defeated, they think,
but they're like a woman underneath a man, circling him.

One molecule-mote-second thinking of God's reversal of comfort
    and pain
is better than any attending ritual. That splinter
of intelligence is substance.
The fire and water themselves:
Accidental, done with mirrors.

(Nicholson, *Mathnawi,* Book V, 420–455)

The Variety of Intelligences in Human Beings

As many kinds as might be marked on a vertical
from the ground to the highest point of the sky:

One intelligence is a steadily burning orb.
One a tiny meteor flickering in and out the atmosphere of Venus.
There is a lantern that looks drunken, barely lighted,
then flaring to the ceiling, blackening the wall.
There is a cold night star. Many sorts
of intelligent fire. One, green, translucent, plant-green.
One a pole moving out from behind an obscurity.

There's not one mind-form everywhere equal, as some have said,
but it is particular intelligences that distort Universal
Intelligence, the ones that use light to hunt with.
The Mind of the Whole does otherwise. It gets a glimpse
of a lovely hunt going on, where God
is Hunter and everything else the hunted. That Mind
sees and tries to quit hunting and completely
be prey. That's the difference.

There's no way to win from where you've gotten yourself.
The queen has your king in danger. When you move out of check,
she takes the rook. Contrive instead
to be near one who serves well.
Figure how to be delivered from your own figuring.
Try to lose. Don't do anything
for power or influence. Run into the mind's fire.
Play this game because you love, and the playing is love.
Beg and cry and come walking on your knees.
Thoughtful supplication won't help.
Joseph's brothers wept, but inside
they were tricky and jealous.

(Nicholson, *Mathnawi,* Book V, 459–476)

78

Why Organize a Universe This Way?

What does not exist looks so handsome.
What does exist, where is it?
An ocean is hidden. All we see is foam,
shapes of dust, spinning, tall as minarets, but I want wind.
Dust can't rise up without wind, I know, but can't I understand
    this
by some way other than induction.

Invisible ocean, wind. Visible foam and dust: This is speech.
Why can't we hear *thought?*
These eyes were born asleep.
Why organize a universe this way?

With the merchant close by a magician measures out
five hundred ells of linen moonlight.
It takes all his money, but the merchant buys the lot.
Suddenly there's no linen, and of course there's no money,
which was his life spent wrongly, and yours.
Say, *Save me, Thou One,* from witches who tie knots
and blow on them. They're tying them again.
Prayers are not enough. You must do something.

Three companions for you: Number one,
what you own. He won't even leave the house
for some danger you might be in. He stays inside.
Number two, your good friend. He at least comes to the funeral.
He stands and talks at the gravesite. No further.

The third companion, what you do, your work,
goes down into death to be there with you,
to help. Take deep refuge
with that companion, beforehand.

(Nicholson, *Mathnawi,* Book V, 1026-1050)

Those You Are With

What is a real connection between people? When the same knowledge
opens a door between them. When the same inner sight exists
in you as in another, you are drawn to be companions.
When a man feels in himself the inmost nature of a woman,
he is drawn to her sexually. When a woman
feels the masculine self of a man within her,
she wants him physically in her.

When you feel the qualities of Gabriel in you, you fly up quickly
like a fledgling not thinking of the ground.
When you feel asinine qualities in you, no matter how you try
to do otherwise, you will head toward the stable.

The mouse is not despicable for its form, which is a helpless victim
to birds of prey, the mouse who loves dark places and cheese
and pistachio nuts and syrup. When the white falcon, though,
has the inner nature of a mouse, it is a disgrace
to all animals. Angelic figures and criminals
shackled head-down in a pit are similar-looking,
same arms, same head. Moses is a bright spirit,
Pharoah disgusting with his sorcery.

Always search for your innermost nature in those you are with.
As rose-oil imbibes from roses.
Even on the grave of a holy man, a holy man lays his face
and hands and takes in light.

(Nicholson, *Mathnawi,* Book VI, 2992–3008)

Learning the Signs of the Zodiac

It's reasonable to be afraid of dying, but love has more courage
than reason. A stone is not so frightened of rain as a clod is.

This is the fifth scroll of the *Mathnawi*. It can help you
find your way like the stars in the signs of the zodiac.
But only a mariner who studies the stars and knows the directions
they lead can use them. To others there's nothing but looking at
    them.
From darkfall to daybreak make yourself familiar with these stars.
Each one is boiling naphtha poured down on demons.
Scorpions to them; to you, good companions.
The Sagittarian bow attacks your enemies. The Aquarian bucket
pours water for your crops. The Piscean fish wrecks
the wandering boat. The truthful Bull
helps with plowing. The Sun-Lion tears the night
to shreds and brings the honor of a glowing redness.

Every existence is poison to some and spirit-sweetness to others.
Be the Friend. Then you can eat from a poison jar
and taste only clear discrimination.

(Nicholson, *Mathnawi*, Book V, 4226–4238)

The Phrasing Must Change

Learn about your inner self from those who know such things,
but don't repeat verbatim what they say.
Zuleika let *everything* be the name of Joseph, from celery seed
to aloes-wood. She loved him so much, she concealed his name
in many different phrases, the inner meanings
known only to her. When she said, *The wax is softening
near the fire,* she meant, My love is wanting me.
Or if she said, *Look, the moon is up,* or *The willow has new leaves,*
or *The branches are trembling,* or *The coriander seeds
have caught fire,* or *The roses are opening,*
or *The king is in a good mood today,* or *Isn't that lucky,*
or *The furniture needs dusting,* or
The water-carrier is here, or *It's almost daylight,* or
These vegetables are perfect, or *The bread needs more salt,*
or *The clouds seem to be moving against the wind,*
or *My head hurts,* or *My headache's better,*
anything she praises, it's Joseph's touch she means,
any complaint, it's his being away.
When she's hungry, it's for him. Thirsty, his name is a sherbet.
Cold, he's a fur. This is what the Friend can do
when one is in such love. Sensual people use the holy names
often, but they don't work for them.
The miracle Jesus did by being the name of God,
Zuleika felt in the name of *Joseph.*

When one is united to the core of another, to speak of that
is to breathe the name *Hu,* empty of self and filled
with love. As the saying goes, *The pot drips what is in it.*
The saffron spice of connecting, laughter.
The onion-smell of separation, crying.
Others have many things and people they love.
This is not the way of Friend and friend.

(Nicholson, *Mathnawi,* Book VI, 4020–4043)